PHILADELPHIA
EAGLES

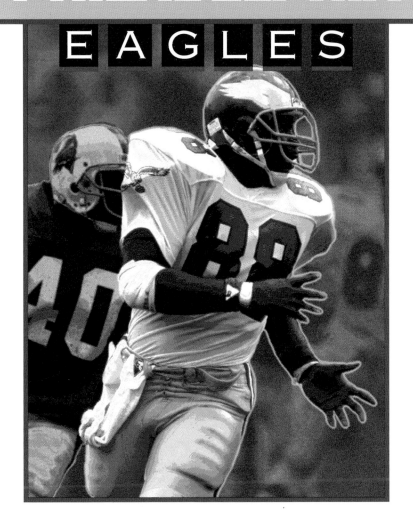

RICHARD RAMBECK

CREATIVE ● EDUCATION INC.

Published by Creative Education, Inc.

123 S. Broad Street, Mankato, Minnesota 56001

Designed by Rita Marshall

Cover illustration by Lance Hidy Associates

Photos by Allsport, Bettmann Archives, Diane Johnson, Duomo,
Focus On Sports, Spectra Action, Sportschrome and Wide World Photos

Library of Congress Cataloging-in-Publication Data

Rambeck, Richard.
  Philadelphia Eagles/Richard Rambeck.
  p.   cm.
  ISBN 0-88682-379-X
  1. Philadelphia Eagles (Football team)—History.   I. Title.
GV956.P44R36   1990
796.332′64′0974811—dc20   90-41206
                                            CIP

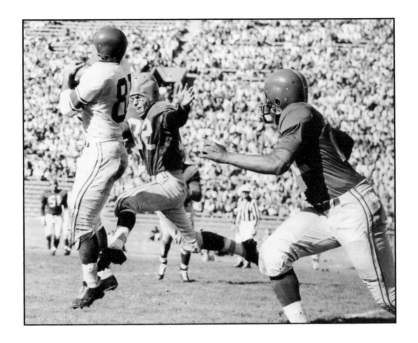

Perhaps no city has played as large a role in American history as Philadelphia. The Declaration of Independence was signed there on July 4, 1776. After the United States won its independence from Great Britain in the Revolutionary War, the Constitution was signed in Philadelphia in 1787. From 1790 to 1800, the place known as the "City of Brotherly Love" served as the capital of the young nation. Philadelphia is also home to Independence Hall, which houses the symbol of our nation's freedom, the Liberty Bell.

In addition to having a rich history and many historical landmarks, Philadelphia is the fifth largest city in the

The Eagles have a long history of success.

Halfback Steve Van Buren led the league by rushing for 832 yards and scoring 110 points.

United States, with more than 1.5 million people. Located on the Delaware River in western Pennsylvania, Philadelphia is also the largest freshwater port in the world.

It is fitting, given Philadelphia's place in American history, that its pro football team has the nickname Eagles, after the symbol of our country. The Philadelphia Eagles played their first season in the National Football League in 1933. The team had been the Frankfort Yellowjackets, but Bert Bell and college friend Lud Wray bought the franchise for $2,800 and moved it to Philadelphia.

Bell wanted to make the Eagles the best team in the NFL, but that didn't happen; the team endured ten straight losing seasons from 1933 to 1942. Bell even took over as coach for a while, but it didn't change the Eagles' fortunes. Despite the heroics of tiny quarterback Davey O'Brien in the late 1930s, the Eagles never finished higher than fourth in the five-team Eastern Division. Frustrated, Bell sold the team in 1941. The new owner was Alexis Thompson, a wealthy steel executive from New York. Thompson hired Earl "Greasy" Neale as coach, and the first part of Philadelphia's championship formula was in place.

In 1944, the Eagles acquired the second part of the formula when they drafted Steve Van Buren, an outstanding running back from Louisiana State University. Van Buren combined with Tommy Thompson, Philadelphia's one-eyed quarterback, and fullback Pete Pihos to give the Eagles one of the best offenses in the league. The Eagles won the Eastern Division three straight years, from 1947 to 1949. The team also won the league title in 1948 and 1949. Van Buren was one of the league's top rushers, Thompson was the NFL passing leader, and Neale was considered perhaps the best coach in the league.

Ron Jaworski rekindled memories of Tommy Thompson.

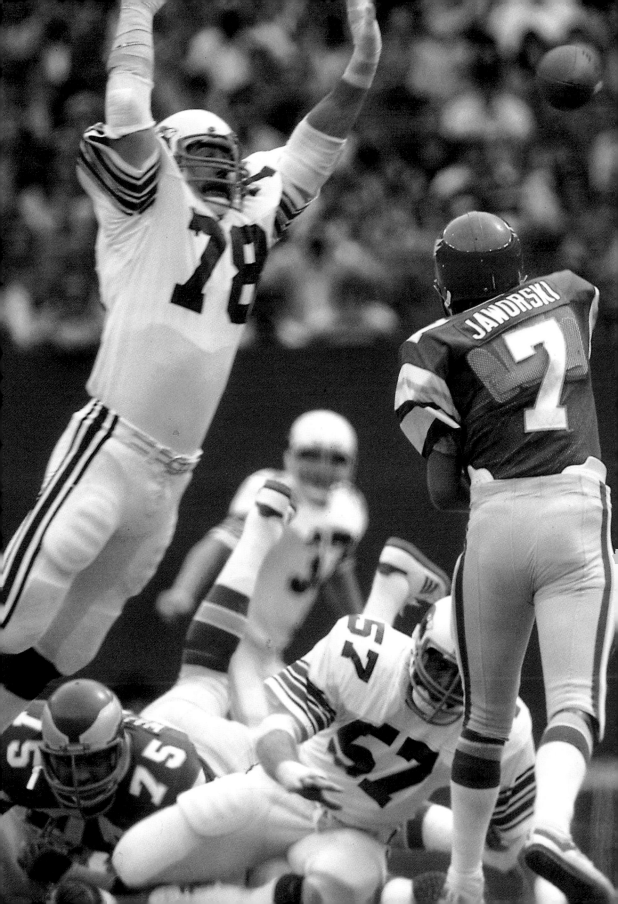

1 9 5 5

Wide receiver Pete Pihos grabbed eleven passes during a contest with the Cardinals.

The Eagles were truly soaring, but their stay at the top of the league ended after the 1949 championship. The team slumped again. Philadelphia spent most of the 1950s in the lower half of the Eastern Division. Van Buren retired, but the Eagles had found a new star, a player who had grown up in Philadelphia.

Chuck Bednarik was different from most football players. How? He was tougher. Injuries, no matter how bad, didn't seem to bother him. Bednarik played with broken bones, torn tendons, and separated shoulders. The durable Bednarik joined the Eagles in 1949 and was a starter at linebacker on Philadelphia's 1949 championship team. As his career progressed, Bednarik also became a center. In many games, he played both ways—as a linebacker on defense and as a center on offense. He became known as the "sixty-minute man" because he rarely came out of the game. In his twelve years in the NFL, Bednarik was named All-Pro, at either linebacker or center, eight times.

In 1958, Bednarik suffered a bad knee injury, so bad that he had to stop playing linebacker. Still the Eagles' center, however, Bednarik was the one who snapped the ball to the new Philadelphia star. Quarterback Norm Van Brocklin came to the Eagles from the Los Angeles Rams. Philadelphia had to give up a first-round draft choice and two starters in a trade for Van Brocklin, but nobody in Philadelphia was complaining. Van Brocklin was that good, and he helped turn the Eagles into winners again.

In 1960, everything fell into place. Van Brocklin couldn't be stopped, and the Eagles soared into first place in the Eastern Division. They won in strange ways, often falling far behind and then rallying to win in the second half. "We trailed at halftime in five games, sometimes by twenty-four points," said wide receiver Tommy McDonald. "But each time between halves, Van Brocklin went to the blackboard, explained what the defense was doing, and we came back to win in the second half." McDonald and fellow receiver Pete Retzlaff caught most of the crucial passes in the Eagles' high-powered offense.

1 9 6 0

Tommy McDonald, who scored thirteen touchdowns during the season, was a key part of the Eagles' offense.

As the season wore on, though, injuries started to haunt the team. Two linebackers were hurt and lost for the season. Coach Buck Shaw was desperate. It was too late to bring a new player onto the team, so he was stuck with what he had. But he had Bednarik, who figured his linebacking days were over. "I never expected it," Bednarik said. "I was sitting on the bench and Buck called me over. 'You're the only guy left,' he told me. 'Get in there, but don't pull any hero stuff.' I played the rest of the game." Bednarik played on both offense and defense for the rest of the season. The Eagles, with Bednarik and cornerback Tom Brookshier leading the defense, won the Eastern Division title. For the first time in eleven years, Philadelphia played for a championship.

The game was at Philadelphia's Franklin Field, and the opponent was the Green Bay Packers, coached by the legendary Vince Lombardi. The Packers, who would win five NFL titles during the 1960s, were loaded with stars on offense, notably quarterback Bart Starr, and defense. The Packers were also fairly young; most of the team's top players were in their mid-twenties. The Eagles, on the other hand, were led by a coach, a quarterback, and a linebacker who were playing their last game with the team: Buck Shaw had announced his retirement, Van

A current Philadelphia star, Keith Jackson (#88), (pages 10–11).

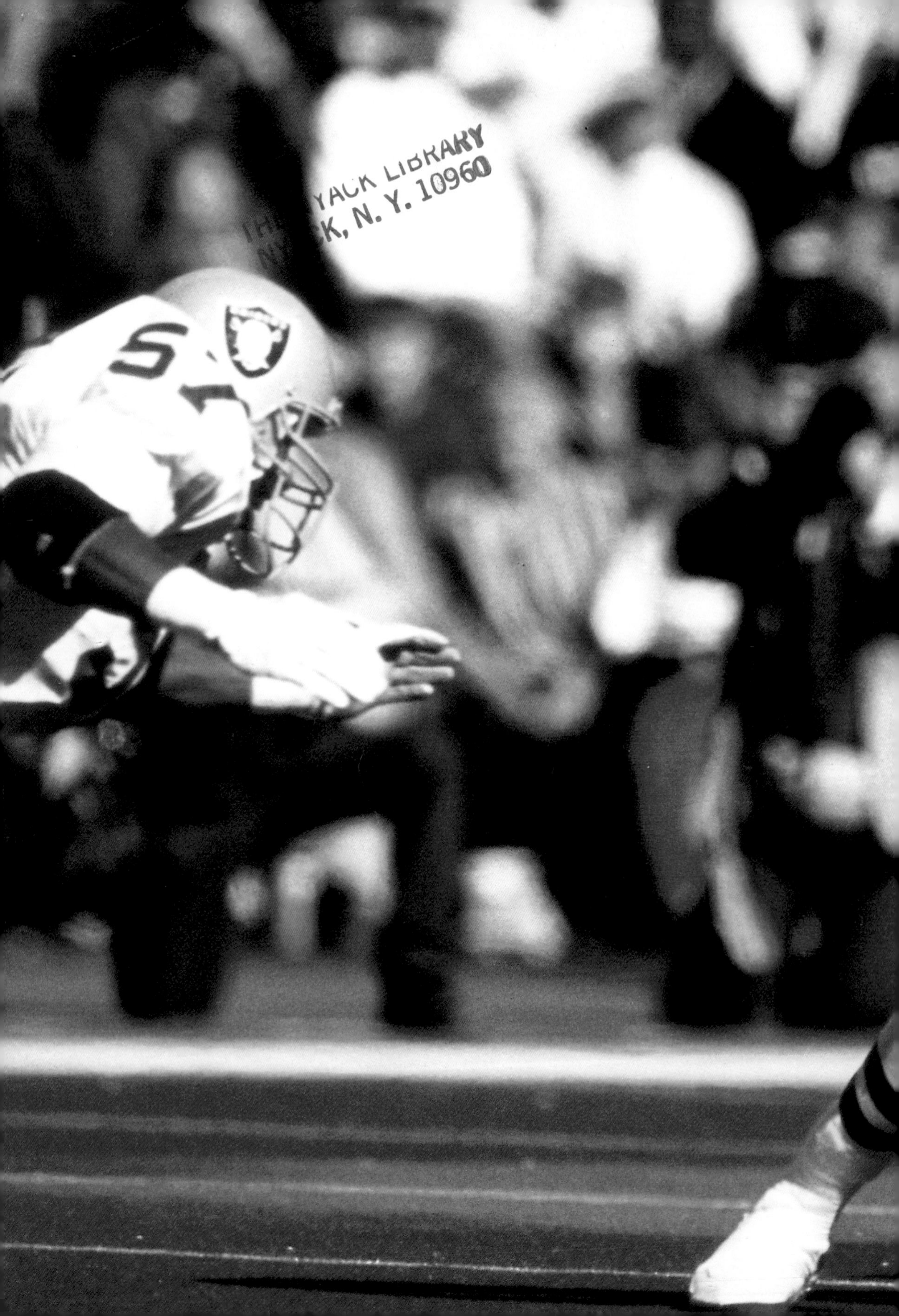

1 9 6 1

Center-linebacker Chuck Bednarik was one of eight Eagles selected for the Pro Bowl.

Brocklin would not return to the Eagles in 1961, and Bednarik was concluding his marvelous twelve-year career.

Bednarik knew he would have to play a good game on both offense and defense for the Eagles to win. "There was no question that I would play both ways against Green Bay," Bednarik said. Once the game started, it was obvious that the Packers were going to have trouble with the Philadelphia defense. "We didn't do anything fancy on defense," Bednarik said. "The Packers were a good team, but we just swarmed all over them."

As the clock wound down in the fourth quarter, the Eagles were holding a 17-13 lead. Starr had one last chance to produce the winning touchdown. In the final minute, Starr moved the Packers into Philadelphia territory. On the game's final play, Starr went back to pass and hit fullback Jim Taylor, who was wide open. Taylor looked like he had a chance to score. He ran down the right sideline and then cut to the middle. But Taylor's journey ended at the ten-yard line. Bednarik came over and made a crushing hit, falling on top of Taylor as the last few seconds ticked off the clock.

"I could see the clock at one corner of Franklin Field," Bednarik said. "I wasn't about to move until it ran out, but he started squirming and shouting at me. But I didn't move until that clock hit the zero mark." When the game ended, Bednarik finally got off Taylor. "OK, Jimmy," Bednarik said, "you can get up now. The game is over."

In the locker room, Buck Shaw paid tribute to Bednarik, who played in fifty-eight of the game's sixty minutes. "We got to hand it to the old pro," Shaw said. "Bednarik's the one that held us together on offense and defense." Even

Bednarik was surprised by what he had done, especially since he was thirty-five years old, the oldest player on the field. "It amazes me when I think about it," he said. "But then, it was mind over matter. We were winning, and that's what was important."

Bednarik was the last man to play both offense and defense for an entire game in the NFL. He ended his pro career just as he had started it in 1949—on a championship team. A few years after he retired, Bednarik was named the best center in the first fifty years of professional football.

Neither Bednarik nor Van Brocklin played for the Eagles in 1961. The team, led by new quarterback Sonny Jurgenson, finished second in the Eastern Division. But the Eagles soon went downhill. Philadelphia eventually traded the talented Jurgenson to the Washington Redskins. Losing suddenly became a habit the Eagles couldn't break. The 1966 team did manage to finish second in the division, but that proved to be the best season for Philadelphia until the end of the 1970s.

1 9 6 7

Although quarterback Norm Snead set club passing records, the Eagles posted a disappointing 6-7-1 record.

VERMEIL AND JAWORSKI

It didn't matter what the Eagles did. They changed coaches. They changed quarterbacks. They even changed the color of their helmets from green to white. None of it made any difference. Players such as receiver Harold Carmichael, center Guy Morriss, tackles Jerry Sisemore and Stan Walters, and safety Randy Logan spent several years with Philadelphia and never knew the thrill of playing for a winning team. Never, that is, until Dick

13

All-Pro linebacker Bill Bergey's play was outstanding in Philadelphia's new 3-4 defense.

Vermeil came along. The Eagles hired Vermeil in February 1976. He had been a successful college coach at UCLA, leading the Bruins to a Rose Bowl victory over Ohio State in 1975.

When Eagle owner Leonard Tose introduced Vermeil as Philadelphia's new coach, it was apparent that Tose believed he had the man who could turn the Eagles around. "I don't want to put our other coaches down," Tose said. "But I'm telling you that this time the Philadelphia fans are getting the real thing—a great coach."

Upon his appointment as head coach, Vermeil called a press conference. "In five years," he said without blinking, "the Eagles will be Super Bowl material." Doubters asked: Who is this guy? Doesn't he know that the Eagles have had only one winning season in the last fifteen years? Of course Vermeil knew, but he didn't care. He knew he could coach the Eagles to victory.

As the Philadelphia coach, Vermeil worked very hard, probably harder than any coach in the NFL. During the season he didn't go home at night; he slept on a cot in his office. But the Eagles needed more than hard work to become winners, and Vermeil knew it. He knew he had to convince the team that it could win. That would be his toughest task, but he had help from a quarterback named Ron Jaworski.

Jaworski came to the Eagles from the Los Angeles Rams in 1977. He brought with him an attitude that didn't accept losing. "When I first got to Philadelphia, I found a bunch of guys shell-shocked from losing," Jaworski said. "They had been through some lean years. They just didn't know what it was like to have fun in football. They were quiet, they kept to themselves. I said, 'Hey, this has got to change.'

Dick Vermeil developed a powerful Eagle offense.

1 9 7 8

*Running back
Wilbert Montgomery
rushed for over
1200 yards.*

I went around patting guys on the back, telling them everything was gonna be cool. It was time for the Eagles to become winners."

Jaworski's new teammates didn't know what to make of him. "I thought he was crazy," said Stan Walters, one of the veterans who had almost grown accustomed to losing. "He had this goofy porkpie hat on, and he was yapping away a mile a minute. Every other quarterback I'd played with had been a loner or very businesslike. Jaworski wasn't like that. He was laughing and yelling and telling us we're going to be winners. We're coming off a 4-10 record, and he's talking about winning a title. Crazy."

But Jaworski wasn't crazy. He, like Vermeil, believed the Eagles could win. Jaworski and Vermeil spent so much time together, people joked that they were Siamese twins. They studied films and figured out ways the Eagles could use Jaworski's rifle arm. Slowly but surely, Jaworski got better and better . . . and so did the Eagles.

In Vermeil's third season as coach, in 1978, the Eagles needed a victory in their final game to do two things: register their first winning season since 1966 and earn a spot in the playoffs. "Twelve years," Vermeil said in the locker room, his voice choked with emotion. "Twelve years since the Eagles have been winners. Well, let me tell you something, gentlemen. You're going to be winners today."

The Eagles went out and defeated the New York Giants. After the game, Jaworski ran back to the locker room screaming, "We're winners! We're winners!" Jaworski then saw Eagles owner Leonard Tose. "Hey, boss! We're winners!" Jaworski yelled, giving Tose a hug. Behind Jaworski was Vermeil. "Congratulations," Tose said to the coach he had called great three years before.

"I couldn't have done it without you," Vermeil said, his head buried on Tose's shoulder. There, in the locker room, owner and coach cried like babies. The Eagles were finally winners. They were also a play-off team, but Atlanta ended Philadelphia's season with a 14-13 comeback win in the first round. Philadelphia also made it to the playoffs in 1979, losing in the second round to Tampa Bay. Vermeil still had one goal left to achieve—winning the Super Bowl.

In 1980, Philadelphia won its first division title since 1960. Jaworski had a great year, and so did veteran running back Wilbert Montgomery, as well as receivers Harold Carmichael and Charlie Smith. The Eagles then defeated Minnesota and Dallas in the playoffs. Five years after he took the Philadelphia coaching job and told everyone that the Eagles would be Super Bowl material in five years, Dick Vermeil had proven himself right; the Eagles were in the Super Bowl.

The Eagles ran out of luck, though, against the Oakland Raiders in Super Bowl XV in New Orleans. The Raiders, behind quarterback Jim Plunkett, won 27-10. "Four years ago," Jaworski said in the locker room after the game, "this team was a doormat. Now we're Super Bowl material. You know how satisfying that is?" Jaworski was named the NFL Player of the Year for leading the Eagles to the Super Bowl.

The future looked bright. The Eagles believed they still hadn't reached their peak. But they had. Vermeil retired

1 9 7 9

Coach Dick Vermeil led his team to an 11-5 record, the Eagles' best showing since 1961.

A swarming defense is a Philadelphia tradition, (pages 18–19).

after the 1982 season, saying he was "burned out." Anyone who knew Vermeil could understand why; it seemed as if he was always working, always trying to make the Eagles better. But the Eagles didn't get better. The winning seasons stopped.

REGGIE WHITE BECOMES MINISTER OF DEFENSE

1 9 8 3

Wide receiver Mike Quick put in a standout performance, leading the league in pass receptions.

Philadelphia had to rebuild to reach championship heights again. That rebuilding process began with a man who would become the Eagles' most dominant defensive player since Chuck Bednarik. When defensive end Reggie White came to the Eagles in 1985, he was already an experienced pro player even though he had never played in the NFL. White had played two years with the Memphis Showboats in the United States Football League. While he was with the Showboats, teammates started calling White the "Minister of Defense." White, who was also a Baptist minister, was the most dominant defensive player in the USFL. When that league folded, White became a Philadelphia Eagle.

Reggie White was something special—a true star. But growing up hadn't been easy for White. "When I was a child, I was always bigger than the other kids," White said. "Kids used to call me 'Bigfoot' or 'Land of the Giant.' They'd tease me and run away. Around seventh grade, I found something I was good at. I could play football, and I could use my size and achieve success by playing within the rules. I remember telling my mother that someday I would be a professional football player and I'd take care of her for the rest of her life."

White also took care of his opponents on the field. He

20

was a complete defensive lineman, one who could rush the passer but also stop running plays. "The so-called men of the game pride themselves on being complete players," White said. "Sacks are great, and they get you elected to the Pro Bowl. But I've always felt that a great defensive lineman has to play the run and the pass equally well."

Offensive linemen just couldn't handle White. He was too big, too strong, and too fast. "He can kill you with his speed," said San Francisco tackle Harris Barton. "But if you overplay it and open up too wide, he'll rush inside, and you're finished. The first thing you have to worry about is his power. If he gets his hands on you, then he's like an offensive lineman. He'll drive you right into the backfield."

1 9 8 6

The Eagles selected running back Keith Byars from Ohio State as their number one draft pick.

Sports Illustrated polled NFL players in 1989, asking them to name the best defensive player in the league. Reggie White was named more than three times as much as any other player in the league; 38 percent of those polled selected him. Teams went to unbelievable lengths to try to keep White under control. The New York Giants even lined up three tight ends on White's side. "Just to give him something to think about," said Giants offensive co-ordinator Ron Ehrhardt. "Just another scheme to control him. Of course, we have other plans for him too."

In 1986, White's second year with the Eagles, the team hired a new coach, Buddy Ryan. Ryan was the assistant coach who made the Chicago Bears the best defensive team in pro football. The Bears won the Super Bowl after the 1985 season, and many gave more credit to Ryan, the defensive coordinator, than to head coach Mike Ditka. A lot of teams would have loved to have Ryan as a head coach, but the Eagles were the ones who got him.

All-Pro quarterback Randall Cunningham.

When Ryan came to Philadelphia, the Eagles were young and in need of direction. White was outstanding on defense, but the Eagles needed to develop talent at other positions. Ryan was particularly interested in a young quarterback, Randall Cunningham, who was six feet five and could throw the ball a mile. Cunningham was a great athlete, but he was unpolished. When he was a child, Cunningham dreamed of playing pro football. His older brother Sam had been a star fullback at the University of Southern California. Sam Cunningham also played several years with the New England Patriots in the NFL. Randall was taller than Sam, but not as strong. He was built to be a quarterback, and that's the position he played in college at the University of Nevada-Las Vegas. Things weren't easy at first; he wasn't an immediate success at UNLV. Still, his family and friends believed in him.

During the summer after his freshman year in college, Cunningham was playing catch with a friend, Tony Gilbert. "Randall threw a ball from one end of the field to the other," said Bruce Cunningham, Randall's older brother. "Tony dove in the end zone and caught it. He came back, breathing hard, and said, 'Randall, one of these days you are going to be the best quarterback in the NFL.' Randall never forgot that."

Cunningham became a star at UNLV, but many people close to him never got a chance to see it happen. Both his parents died during his sophomore year. Gilbert, Cunningham's best friend while growing up, died of cancer. Those deaths made Cunningham more determined than ever to be a pro football star.

Reggie White was selected Pro Bowl MVP after recording four quarterback sacks in the game.

Clockwise: Heath Sherman, Keith Jackson, Eric Allen, Reggie White.

The Eagles took Cunningham in the second round of the 1985 draft. He didn't play much his rookie year. But when Ryan became head coach, Cunningham started to see more playing time. In 1987 Cunningham threw twenty-three touchdown passes, the third most in the National Football Conference. He also led the team in rushing with more than five hundred yards. Also in 1987 Reggie White had twenty-one sacks, the most in the NFL. Wide receiver Mike Quick caught eleven touchdown passes, the second most in the NFL. The Eagles were building a championship-caliber team again.

1 9 8 8

Keith Jackson was selected as The Sporting News' *NFL Rookie of the Year for his sensational debut.*

Philadelphia won the NFC Eastern Division title in 1988 behind Cunningham, who was chosen to play in the Pro Bowl, and White, who led the league in sacks again with eighteen. Rookie tight end Keith Jackson caught an amazing eighty-one passes and joined Cunningham in the Pro Bowl. Running back Keith Byars showed his versatility by scoring ten touchdowns, six on runs and four via pass receptions. Byars, who had seventy-two catches, was also one of the league's top receivers. Philadelphia's best wide receiver, Mike Quick, broke his leg and missed most of the season, but second-year receiver Cris Carter filled in with some spectacular catches.

Philadelphia had lots of stars, but it was the athletic Cunningham everybody was talking about. "Randall is a talent, a great natural athlete and a great leader on the field," said Philadelphia owner Norman Braman. "He's made himself what he is. Randall's teammates believe he can do anything."

Ryan showed how much he believed in Cunningham's

The dependable Anthony Toney, (pages 26–27).

Multi-talented quarterback Randall Cunningham led the Eagles in rushing for the third straight year.

ability by basically giving his quarterback control over the offense. "Buddy came to me and said, 'It's your offense. If it doesn't work, it's going to be your fault.' I don't mind that at all. Let the pressure be on me, not Buddy. Buddy has given me a home."

Why would Ryan give Cunningham that kind of responsibility? "First of all, he's the best athlete ever to play the position," Ryan said. "I call him the Boss so the other guys can hear it. It's his offense. I want him to realize that. He doesn't want to be good. He wants to be great. And he is willing to work to be that way."

In training camp before the 1989 season, Cunningham was executing a passing drill to perfection. One defensive back said to another, "They want us to try to stop this?" The other defensive back said, "Yeah, but they don't expect us to." The Eagles didn't expect anybody to stop Cunningham. Neither did Cunningham.

"I'm an impact player. Impact. That is what separates guys like me. It's a proud feeling," Cunningham said. "I want people to understand, whether it's practice or a game, I don't hold anything back. I've been given the talent to run and throw and kick. The way Buddy has built me up, the pressure is definitely on me."

The Eagles put the pressure on other NFC East teams for most of 1989. They stayed in first place in the division until things started coming apart late in the year. Cunningham and the offense had trouble moving the ball consistently. Then Doug Scovil, the assistant coach Cunningham was closest to, died of a heart attack after a practice.

But the Eagles were tough. Although they didn't win their division, they did earn a playoff spot as a wildcard

Cunningham's favorite target, Keith Jackson.

Wide receiver Ron Johnson.

The Eagle defense.

team. Playing at home against the Los Angeles Rams in the first round of the playoffs, Philadelphia fell behind 14-0 in the first quarter and couldn't catch up. The season ended, but hopes for the future were high.

The Eagles' stars—Cunningham and White—are both in their twenties and in the prime of their careers. So are Keith Jackson, Keith Byars, and Cris Carter. In addition, White isn't the only Pro Bowl-quality defensive lineman playing for Philadelphia. Jerome Brown, who lines up opposite White, has become one of the most feared pass rushers in the game. Young cornerback Eric Allen also has shown star potential.

These players represent a successful rebuilding process that has brought the Eagles back up to the level of the 1980 Super Bowl team. Now, with Ryan leading them, the Eagles are championship contenders, and they figure to be flying high for years to come.

1 9 9 0

Reggie White led the Eagles to a wildcard spot in the NFC playoffs.